TEEN MENTAL HEALTH™

self-image and
eating disorders

Rita Smith, Vanessa Baish,
Edward Willett, and
Stephanie Watson

ROSEN
PUBLISHING®

New York

Published in 2013 by The Rosen Publishing Group, Inc.
29 East 21st Street, New York, NY 10010

First Edition

Library of Congress Cataloging-in-Publication Data

Self-image and eating disorders/Rita Smith...[et al.].—1st ed.
    p. cm.—(Teen mental health)
Includes bibliographical references and index.
ISBN 978-1-4488-6894-0 (library binding)
1. Eating disorders in adolescence—Psychological aspects—
Juvenile literature. 2. Eating disorders in adolescence—
Treatment—Juvenile literature. 3. Body image in
adolescence—Juvenile literature. I. Smith, Rita P.
RJ506.E18S45 2013
616.85'2600835—dc23

2012003030

Manufactured in the United States of America

CPSIA Compliance Information: Batch #S12YA: For further information, contact Rosen Publishing, New York, New York,
at 1-800-237-9932.

contents

chapter one

Body Image and Self-Image

Do you see the reflection of a happy, healthy young person when you look in the mirror? Or someone you automatically cut down as being too fat, too short, or too ugly? Have you ever thought your whole life would be better if you were thinner and more attractive? These feelings are the result of a negative body image.

In today's society, body image is more than just the mental picture you have of what your body looks like. For many, body image is also a reflection of how they feel about themselves and their lives. People with a negative body image believe that if they don't look right, their personality, intelligence, social skills, or capabilities also aren't right. They think that if they fix their bodies, all their other problems will disappear. This can result in unhealthy weight management practices and an unhealthy relationship with food.

Your body image is influenced by many different things. It is influenced by family, friends, and a culture that is obsessed with weight, body shape, dieting, and food. All people have negative thoughts and feelings about their body at some point in their life. But

For teens, body image is a big part of self-image. Having a negative self-image makes it more likely that teens will focus on their problems instead of their positive traits.

when it becomes more than a passing concern, when people base their happiness and self-worth on what they eat, how often they exercise, and how much they weigh, they are suffering from a negative body image. This outlook causes people to believe that all their experiences in life are affected by their appearance and body weight.

Even worse, when this preoccupation with food and weight turns into an obsession, it can result in a full-blown eating disorder. According to the National Eating Disorders Association (NEDA), more than eleven million people in the United States suffer from an eating disorder such as bulimia nervosa or anorexia nervosa, and another twenty-five million are battling compulsive (binge) eating disorder.

Negative Body Image and Teens

Teen model and actress Dakota Fanning attends a fashion show. Many experts blame the fashion industry for promoting thinness as the ideal, which can often lead teens to develop eating disorders.

The problems surrounding body image can be especially difficult for teens. Adolescence is a time when you may feel confused about the changes happening to your body. These changes are a natural part of growing up, but they can make you feel out of control and unhappy with your appearance. As a result, you may turn to unhealthy eating habits, which can lead to a serious eating disorder. This can seriously damage your physical and emotional health.

Nobody is born with a negative body

image. It is something that you learn, something that develops over time. As you grow older, your experiences are shaped by the different messages you get from society. And those messages often connect personal success and happiness with being thin and beautiful. If people feel they don't measure up to those ideals of success, they tend to disregard any other real accomplishments. Having a negative body image can seriously distort the way you look at yourself and your life. This negative image can be very dangerous if it's not addressed. The good news is, because a negative body image is something you learn, it can also be unlearned.

If you work on learning to love and respect your body right now, you'll have the time, energy, and willpower to focus on the most important part of your being—who you are inside.

Improving Your Self-Image

Self-image is how you see yourself from the inside. This includes how you see yourself physically and how you think others see you, what kind of person you think you are, what kind of personality you think you have, if you think others like you and if you like yourself. Your self-image affects your self-confidence. Your self-confidence is what you project to the outside world and how other people see you. If you have a good self-image, you will also project self-confidence.

To find out what your self-image is, it is best to begin by looking at how you see yourself. To build your self-image, you have to start with the reality of who you are.

As you begin to examine your self-image, ask these questions:

- Do you like who you are?
- Do you believe in yourself?
- Do you think you can do the things that you want to do?
- Do you like the things that happen in your life?
- Do you feel that you have any control over your life and how others see you?

Self-esteem is how you feel about yourself, your accomplishments, talents, and possibilities. If you have good self-esteem, you will have confidence in yourself and project a positive self-image.

- Do you think that you are talented and valuable?
- Do you like your body, or do you constantly compare your body to the bodies of others?
- Do you have positive, supportive relationships with your family and friends?
- Do you feel valued by them and accepted as who you really are?

If you answered no to most or all of these questions, you probably have a poor self-image. If this is the case, you are definitely not alone. Most people experience some form of a poor self-image, no matter how sure of themselves they may seem.

To conquer your doubts about yourself and build and manage your self-image, you first need to change the fundamental way you see and talk about yourself. As your self-image starts to improve, your self-confidence will reflect it.

This book will describe some of the common eating disorders that affect young people today and how to work toward changing both your negative body image and your self-image.

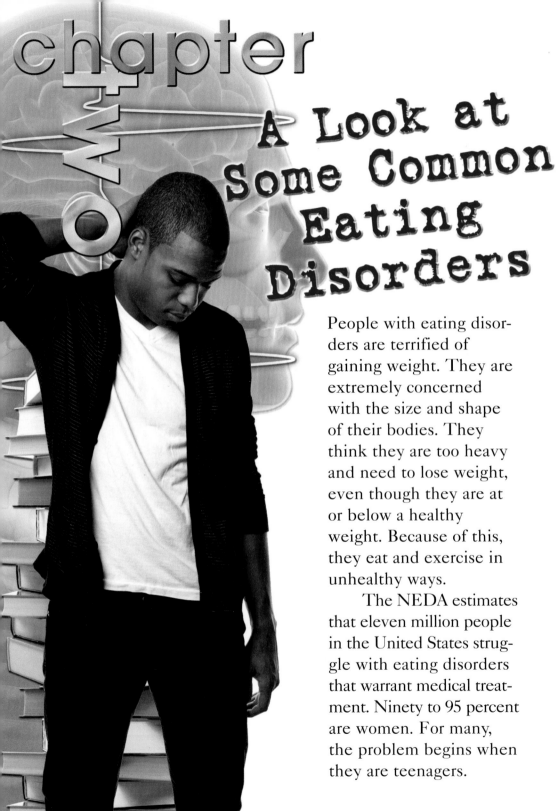

chapter two

A Look at Some Common Eating Disorders

People with eating disorders are terrified of gaining weight. They are extremely concerned with the size and shape of their bodies. They think they are too heavy and need to lose weight, even though they are at or below a healthy weight. Because of this, they eat and exercise in unhealthy ways.

The NEDA estimates that eleven million people in the United States struggle with eating disorders that warrant medical treatment. Ninety to 95 percent are women. For many, the problem begins when they are teenagers.

If it becomes severe, an eating disorder can take over a person's life. Unless that person gets help—and wants help—that person may die. As reported by Anorexia Nervosa and Related Eating Disorders, Inc. (ANRED), 20 percent of people with a serious eating disorder die if they don't get treatment. With treatment, that number declines to 2 to 3 percent.

An eating disorder is a complicated psychological, emotional, and physical problem. Cultural influences can also contribute to an eating disorder. Women experience a lot of pressure from society to be thin and attractive. Some believe this is the reason more women suffer from eating disorders than men. Still, the number of males who have an eating disorder is increasing.

The two main eating disorders are anorexia nervosa and bulimia nervosa. Compulsive eating (also referred to as binge eating disorder) is also a serious problem. Compulsive exercise is currently classified as a serious eating disorder–related problem, and many experts believe the number of people suffering from it is growing. Compulsive exercise is also called exercise bulimia or exercise addiction.

Each of these four disorders is a different type of behavior, but most people with eating disorders suffer from symptoms that fall into more than one category. In other words, many people have symptoms of anorexia and bulimia, or bulimia and exercise addiction, or any combination of these four disorders.

Anorexia Nervosa

Anorexia nervosa is usually shortened to anorexia. Although the word "anorexia" means "loss of appetite," the opposite is true. Those with anorexia are hungry all the time. Their weight is at least 15 percent below average for their height and age. They are starving themselves, sometimes to death. But those with anorexia fear putting on weight and often see themselves as heavier than they really are. Anorexia causes many physical problems. Because the body has so little fat, it can't maintain a normal body temperature. As a result, fine hairs, called lanugo, grow all over the body to try to keep it warm. People with anorexia are frequently cold, even in summer. Young women with anorexia suffer from amenorrhea, which means that menstrual periods stop. Near-starvation and the resulting lack of calcium may cause osteoporosis later in life. Starvation also weakens the heart, which can develop a slow or irregular beat. Loss of fluids can cause dehydration. Dehydration can lead to an electrolyte imbalance in the body, causing death.

Anorexia also causes emotional problems. Because people who have anorexia tend to isolate themselves from family and friends, they

Being very afraid of gaining weight, obsessing about every bite of food that you eat, and worrying about eating too many calories may be warning signs that you have anorexia.

may suffer from depression. Lack of food can harm the person's ability to think straight and concentrate. It can also cause a person to feel irritable, unhappy, and pessimistic most of the time.

Bulimia Nervosa

Bulimia nervosa, or bulimia, is characterized by binge and purge cycles. Bingeing is eating a large amount of food in a short amount of time. Purging is when a person tries to rid the body of the food by vomiting, using laxatives to bring on a bowel movement, abusing diuretics to increase urination, and abusing drugs that induce vomiting. Some people exercise excessively to rid the body of the calories.

Bulimia causes many health problems as well. These include dry skin and hair, brittle nails, or bleeding gums. The teeth develop cavities or ragged edges from stomach acids brought up by frequent vomiting. Vomiting also puts tremendous strain on the

Bulimia involves cycles of binge eating and purging. People who have bulimia may purge once or several times each day, which can lead to dangerous effects on the body.

stomach and esophagus. When the lining of the esophagus breaks down, an ulcer develops. Purging gets rid of food before nutrients are absorbed. Without these nutrients, the body can suffer from malnutrition.

In addition, repeated use of laxatives can cause painful constipation (an inability to have bowel movements). Abusing diuretics can cause dehydration. Using ipecac syrup to induce vomiting is extremely dangerous and can cause congestive heart failure and death.

Bulimia can cause the same emotional problems that people with anorexia develop. Because people who suffer from bulimia keep their binge/purge cycles a secret, they can feel isolated and alone and suffer from depression. The ANRED reported that 50 percent of those who suffer from anorexia develop bulimia or bulimia-like signs. About one million of the eleven million people who suffer from anorexia and bulimia are male.

Compulsive Eating (Binge Eating Disorder)

Compulsive eaters (sometimes called compulsive overeaters) are people who eat in response to psychological stress. In doing so, they eat when they're not hungry. Like those with bulimia, compulsive eaters go on food binges. Some compulsive eaters graze, eating many times during the day or night. People who compulsively overeat may wish to lose weight, but they do not purge food from their bodies.

Compulsive eating is psychologically damaging because people use food as a way to deal with uncomfortable feelings. Because they may not feel safe expressing sadness, anger, or other emotions, they eat as a way to find comfort. Also, most people with this disorder are over-weight and may be at risk for other health problems, such as heart disease and diabetes. Being overweight alone does not always cause health problems, but it can be a problem when combined with an inactive lifestyle.

Obesity

Obesity, the condition of having an excessive amount of body fat, has become such a serious concern that health professionals have begun to attach the "E" word to it: epidemic. In 2010, a report from the Organization for Economic Cooperation and Development revealed that the United States is the fattest nation among thirty-three countries with advanced economies. Two-thirds of people in the United States are overweight or obese and about a third—more than seventy-two million—are obese. The ANRED reported that about 15 percent of U.S. teen girls and almost 14 percent of teen boys are obese. Some reasons for obesity are eating too much fast food or food with lots of sugar and fat, and a lack of exercise.

Orthorexia Nervosa

According to the NEDA, people suffering from orthorexia nervosa are obsessed with healthy eating. In fact, the term "orthorexia nervosa" means "fixation on healthy eating." People with orthorexia usually start out by trying to eat more healthy foods, but they become fixated on the quality and purity of their diet. They may develop rigid rules about what they can and cannot eat, such as refusing to eat anything that contains sugar, salt, caffeine, alcohol, wheat, gluten, yeast, soya, corn, and dairy. The NEDA reports, "Eventually, food choices become so restrictive, with both variety and calories, that health suffers—an ironic twist for a person so completely dedicated to healthy eating."

Compulsive Exercise

Compulsive exercise, also known as exercise addiction, is characterized by using exercise to get rid of calories. This behavior is also known as exercise bulimia because the person is using exercise to purge calories from his or her system. The compulsive exerciser might also eat compulsively; restrict food; throw up; and/or take laxatives, diet pills, or other drugs—or any combination of these.

Compulsive exercise is also a bit different from other eating disorders: it can be a lot easier to hide. If a person stops eating, his or her parents and friends will probably become worried. But because exercise is usually a positive, worthwhile activity, people who stick to an exercise routine are often praised for their discipline. The behavior that wins compliments may actually be harmful. When exercise takes over your life, when it isolates you, when it becomes the sole focus of your thoughts, it has become unhealthy.

Athletes and Eating Disorders

Many teen athletes, anxious and unsure about the relationship between food, weight, and performance, make unhealthy eating choices. Too often, these athletes have extremely limited diets and weight-loss "secrets," which become patterns of deprivation that they cannot stop without help. The eating disorders anorexia nervosa and bulimia nervosa are the most extreme examples of these patterns. These disorders are not fads, bad habits, or ways of expressing personality. Anorexia and bulimia are categorized by health professionals as psychiatric illnesses that require medical and psychiatric or behavioral treatments until the body recovers

Some athletes have compulsive exercise disorder because they want to lose weight and maintain what may be an unrealistic body image. Compulsive exercisers overtrain their bodies, causing injury to their joints, bones, muscles, and cartilage.

and the symptoms go away. The pressures of competition in sports; the emphasis in the U.S. media on being thin; and family, peer, or personal problems can put athletes at risk for developing eating disorders.

For some athletes, bulimia can cause a condition that doctors call the female athlete triad. The word "triad" refers to the three health problems that occur together in many female athletes: disordered eating, loss of menstrual periods, and loss of bone mass. Any one of these conditions can signal that the body's essential nutrients and tissues are being raided, usually by a combination of starvation and overexercising. When all three conditions appear at the same time, it is a health emergency. Experts aren't sure exactly how many women have the female athlete triad.

MYTHS AND FACTS

Myth: Only girls worry about and feel badly about their bodies and self-image.

Fact: According to the organization Anorexia Nervosa and Related Eating Disorders, 10 percent of individuals who have anorexia and bulimia are male.

Myth: People with eating disorders just need to control what they eat by having more willpower and they will get better.

Fact: Eating disorders are medical and psychological illnesses that need treatment by doctors and therapists to be overcome. They are not a choice or a habit.

Myth: When you have an eating disorder, all your body changes that result from them can be reversed.

Fact: Eating disorders can damage organs such as the heart, liver, esophagus, and kidneys permanently.

chapter three

Signs and Causes of Eating Disorders

It's important to remember that the symptoms of eating disorders such as anorexia, bulimia, compulsive eating, and compulsive exercise can be interchangeable. Some of the general warning signs to watch for in yourself is if you are doing the following:

- Constantly thinking about the size and shape of your body
- Constantly thinking about how much you weigh and repeatedly weighing yourself

19

Signs that someone has an eating disorder include refusing to eat, eating alone, denying hunger, making excuses for not eating, and weighing himself or herself excessively.

- Constantly thinking about food, cooking, and eating
- Eating only certain foods in specific and limited amounts
- Wanting to eat alone and feeling uncomfortable eating with other people
- Not feeling good about yourself unless you are thin but never being satisfied with how thin you are
- Feeling that you should exercise more, no matter how much you already exercise
- Feeling competitive about dieting and wanting to be the thinnest or the smallest
- Keeping a list of what foods are OK to eat
- Taking diet pills or abusing laxatives and/or diuretics
- Continuing to diet, even after you are thin
- Purposely losing lots of weight very quickly
- Forcing yourself to throw up
- No longer having your monthly period

- Having severe mood swings
- Alternating between strict dieting and overeating

People who suffer from a negative body image are more likely to have an eating disorder, too. Keep in mind that you don't have to have every symptom on this list to suffer from a negative body image or to have an eating disorder. If some of these signs seem familiar to you, please consider speaking to a trusted adult and getting help.

Having negative feelings about food can seriously affect not only how you eat but also how you interact with your friends, family, and everyone else around you. Your unhealthy relationship with food can harm both your body and your emotions.

Effects of Anorexia on the Body

There are two types of anorexia. People with anorexia either diet and/or exercise constantly to keep their weight down or binge eat and then purge it to avoid gaining weight. Anorexia can lead to these effects on your body:

- Weight loss
- Feeling cold all the time
- Lanugo—a fine hair that grows all over your body
- Disruption or loss of monthly menstruation (your period)
- Feeling tired and/or weak
- Fainting
- Headaches

21

- Pasty complexion
- Yellow palms and soles of feet (due to nutrient imbalance)
- Heart problems
- Infertility (the inability to have children)

Effects of Bulimia on the Body

Bulimia involves cycles of bingeing—as many as five thousand calories or more at once—and then purging the food by vomiting or using drugs such as laxatives or diuretics. People with bulimia may purge once or several times a day. Bingeing and purging can have devastating effects on the body.

People who have bulimia may be hard to spot because their weight may not be much higher or lower than average. The most obvious sign that someone has bulimia is that he or she disappears after meals, usually going into the bathroom. You may see the person purge by strict dieting, fasting, vigorous exercise, vomiting, or using laxatives and diuretics. Bulimics are preoccupied with body weight, constantly getting on the scale.

These are some of the physical side effects of bulimia:

- Frequent complaints about feeling dizzy, light-headed, or faint
- Bruised or callused knuckles and fingers from sticking fingers down the throat to induce vomiting
- Swollen cheeks, giving the face a puffy look
- Sore throat; sore and swollen glands in the neck
- Dry skin, brittle hair, and obvious hair loss

- Lanugo growing on the face, back, and arms
- Dental problems, including tooth and gum decay
- Heartburn and bloating
- Frequent headaches and complaints of being cold
- Tingling in the hands, feet, and face and irregular or slow heartbeat caused by low potassium or other vitamin deficiencies
- Depression and/or sudden mood swings
- Long-term effects may include loss of tooth enamel, arthritis, osteoporosis (a disease that causes bones to weaken and break), back and joint pain, poor circulation, heart problems, sleep problems, and fatigue

Effects of Binge Eating on the Body

When someone binge eats regularly, that person's weight can balloon to a very unhealthy level. And when a person has eaten sparingly for a long time and then eats a huge amount of food in a short period of time, a binge can be fatal.

The body's reaction to continual overeating is the opposite of what happens in anorexic or bulimic eating disorders. There are many changes to the body that take place when a person constantly overeats. These are a few:

- Weight gain
- Feeling warm or hot much of the time
- Fast or irregular heart rate, high blood pressure,

hormone imbalances, and possibly raised cholesterol levels. These conditions are common in over-weight people and could lead to serious heart disease.

• Joint pain, breathing difficulty, and poor circulation caused by the additional stress placed on the body by excess weight

• Stomach and intestinal problems

• Exhaustion, weakness, and dizziness. These are brought on by stress, nutritional imbalances, fast heart rate, and high blood

When a person is overweight or obese, he or she can develop breathing problems, joint problems, fatty liver disease, diabetes, and high blood pressure, among other conditions.

pressure. Excess weight and increased digestive activity from eating too much place greater pressure on the binge eater's body.

Effects of Compulsive Exercise Disorder on the Body

People who have anorexia and bulimia in addition to compulsive exercise disorder don't eat enough to compensate for the amount of exercise they do. This puts a lot of strain on their bodies. The combination of not eating enough and exercising too much over a long period of time can permanently damage internal organs and bone structure. Eventually, if you're combining starvation and exercise, you could die.

If you're exercising too often, especially if you're not eating enough, you could see any of these effects on your body:

- Dehydration, if you're not getting enough fluids
- Fatigue, insomnia, and depression
- Injuries to the joints, bones, muscles, and cartilage
- Loss of menstruation

These eating disorders are very dangerous and can cause permanent physical and emotional damage if they are not diagnosed and treated. If you think you might have one or more of these disorders, or if you suspect that a family member or friend may have an eating disorder, find help as quickly as possible. Remember that you are not alone. You can talk to someone you trust, such as a friend, a teacher, a coach, your parents, a sibling, a guidance counselor, or your doctor.

What Causes Eating Disorders?

Medical professionals have learned a great deal about the symptoms and side effects of eating disorders in the past few decades, but they still don't understand why one person develops an eating disorder while another person with the same background does not. The true cause of eating disorders—if there is a single cause—has yet to be discovered.

It would be easy to believe that eating disorders are all about food, but that isn't the case. Eating behavior is only one part of a complex mystery. The way people with eating disorders eat—or don't eat— is the outward symptom of their inner problems and turmoil.

Despite the differences in the way people develop and experience eating disorders, these people do have certain things in common. The need to be perfect, the need to meet unreasonably high expectations, and the need to feel in control of at least one aspect of their lives are some of the forces that drive the development of eating disorders.

Some Outside Pressures

You may feel a huge pressure to be thin and do well in everything you try, from school to sports. Especially if you're already struggling with internal anxieties and self-doubt, these outside pressures can make you even more vulnerable to developing an eating disorder.

Television, movies, and magazines all promote this unnatural "thin" image. The models are rail thin with not an ounce of fat or a smudge of cellulite on their bodies. Seeing these images constantly can make you have negative feelings about yourself because you don't look this way. In fact, very few people in the world are as thin as models. That type of body is almost impossible to achieve.

Some people become anorexic or bulimic because they believe being skinny is the only way they will be accepted or loved. They literally starve themselves nearly to death trying to meet someone else's unrealistic expectations for body size and shape.

Other People

You draw important information about who you are and how you should behave through contact with others. This information comes perhaps most powerfully from your parents. Your parents may take more control over your life than is necessary or healthy. Young people who have anorexia, for example, are usually the children of controlling parents. They are obedient children and are not likely to rebel. Other parents may not take any control over their child's life, leaving him or her to grow up without any support. Some parents may be emotionally, sexually, or physically abusive. In all these cases, you do not experience a healthy family life and you might turn to food to manage the dysfunction.

You draw other cues about yourself from siblings, friends, teachers, coaches, guidance counselors, and others who become important in your life. If you try to fit into a clique at school or match the academic or athletic achievements of a popular person at school and fail, you may become depressed, and that can pave the way for an eating disorder. If your brother or sister is great at sports or does well in school, he or she may be held up to you as an example. The comparison not only lowers your self-esteem, but it also sets up a rivalry in which you may believe you're doomed to failure because you do not think that you are as talented as your sibling.

The influences key people in your life have on you can be positive or negative. The influence a strong, positive role model might have on you could turn out to be two-sided. Following the lead of an inspirational or extremely talented person could make you more ambitious and improve your abilities. On the other hand, trying to live up to someone's high-achieving example and falling short could badly damage an already fragile self-image.

In the same way, negative influences can cut both ways. You might look at someone whom you feel is a poor role model and decide not to be like her or him. Or you

Some teens who have anorexia have controlling parents and become very defensive about their eating habits. By denying their hunger, they reaffirm that they have taken control of their own lives. In reality, they are harming their bodies.

might think that person is having more fun than you are and you may copy the person.

The Gene Connection

Researchers have found that some eating disorders, such as anorexia, tend to run in families. There may be genes (segments of DNA, found on chromosomes, that determine the inheritance of particular traits from your mother and father) that can make you more likely to develop an eating disorder than someone else. But just because your mother or sister has an eating disorder doesn't mean that you will definitely have one.

Emotions and Self-Esteem

Eating disorders often begin because of emotional reasons. Low self-esteem and low self-worth are common in people who have eating disorders. So are perfectionism and obsessive-compulsive behaviors. People who have eating disorders try to use food to fill their emotional needs or to ease their loneliness.

Three of the biggest factors in people who have eating disorders are low self-esteem, poor or unrealistic body image, and self-image. "Self-esteem" is how you feel about yourself, your accomplishments, talents, and possibilities. In all three of these areas, how you see yourself may not be the same as how the rest of the world sees you.

People with eating disorders can't seem to see their own good points because of low self-esteem. They don't value themselves as much as they value those around

Some people with eating disorders use food to fill the emptiness or unhappiness in their lonely lives.

them. The desire to match an unrealistic body image can become so great that it triggers an eating disorder.

The Idea of Perfection and a Need for Control

For those with anorexia or bulimia, not eating is a way of controlling a world they feel is out of control. For binge eaters, eating is a way to avoid dealing with how they feel. They use food to help cope with stress, to take away the pain in their lives, and to give them comfort.

You need to accept yourself for who you are, with strengths and flaws like any human being. The trouble starts when you lose track of how to balance what you can achieve against what you cannot.

10 Great Questions to Ask a Guidance Counselor

1. How do I learn to like who I am?

2. What can I do to feel comfortable in my body and to like my body?

3. How can I find a therapist who will work with me?

4. How can I change my eating habits?

5. What things can I do to feel less stress in my life?

6. How can I stop being self-critical about myself and my body?

7. Do I have an eating disorder if all I want to do is exercise all the time? Isn't exercise healthy?

8. How can I find people who will support me and accept me for who I really am?

9. Can I take medication, and what effect will it have on me?

10. What is a good weight for my height?

chapter four

Getting Help for Eating Disorders

What happens after you are diagnosed with an eating disorder varies, depending on how severe the disorder is, your physical condition, and how involved you are in your own recovery process. To be successful, treatments must address both the physical and psychological aspects of the eating disorder. People with severe eating disorders may require hospitalizations, while others might recover with outpatient therapy. Some people may be helped by medication, while others might do well with a strong nutritional plan.

Support from Family and Friends

Although recovery can only begin when you accept your situation and decide to change, you can't do it alone. Successful recovery takes the understanding and support of everyone around you—especially your family and friends. Just as personal relationships can be among the

A successful recovery from an eating disorder begins with you, but it must also include the encouragement and support of your family and friends. Talking with a therapist and a family member can help you understand the issues that caused your disorder.

causes of eating disorders, they can also be an important part of the recovery process.

Finding and confronting the root causes of an eating disorder are difficult and painful processes, and you shouldn't act alone. Medical care and counseling, self-help groups, and your family and friends are all important parts of the recovery process.

When Medical Help Is Necessary

The first and most important concern in treating an eating disorder, especially anorexia and bulimia, is to make sure your body is healthy. Dehydration (not having enough liquids in the body), starvation (not having enough nutrients in the body), and electrolyte imbalances (too much or not enough of certain chemicals in the body) can cause serious health problems or even death.

You may be put in a hospital if you:

- Have lost 30 percent of your body weight or more over a period of three months
- Have a severe metabolic disturbance. This means that your digestive process and the way your body accepts and uses nutrients have been upset. Lack of important nutrients such as potassium, calcium, iron, and others can cause permanent damage to your body in a very short time.
- Have been diagnosed with severe depression or are considered a suicide risk. Staying in a hospital can protect your life until your doctors and therapist help you turn the disorder around.

- Have been on a binge-and-purge cycle that becomes severe enough to need immediate medical help
- Have damage to your heart, liver, or kidneys or other medical problems due to long-term starvation from anorexia

While you're in the hospital, you may have behavioral therapy, family education, group therapy, or medication to help you get better.

Treatment Using Medication

Medication is often a successful part of eating disorder treatment. No magic pill or potion exists that will relieve eating disorder symptoms or get rid of the disorder altogether, but there are a few medications that can be helpful.

Because depression is a common part of eating disorders, doctors may sometimes prescribe drugs called antidepressants. Antidepressants can be used to help bulimia and binge eating disorder patients recover, especially if they don't respond well to therapy alone. The most common antidepressants used to treat these eating disorders are the selective serotonin reuptake inhibitors (SSRIs). These SSRIs include Prozac, Zoloft, Paxil, Luvox, Lexapro, and Effexor. Binge eaters may also benefit from weight-loss drugs such as Xenical. There aren't any drugs that have been shown to help treat anorexia, although behavioral treatments can be effective.

Therapy for Eating Disorders

Therapy is basically talking to someone—either alone or in a group—who can help you come to terms with the thoughts that led to the eating disorder to overcome them. Your therapist can also study other issues that may be involved in your eating disorder, such as depression.

Many treatment programs are based on cognitive behavior therapy. Cognition is the process of knowing, including perception, memory, and judgment. Cognitive behavior therapy can help you understand why you developed an eating disorder and learn how to come to terms with the issues that caused it. Several types of therapy are used to treat eating disorders, including the following:

Working individually with a psychologist is one method of treating an eating disorder or underlying feelings of depression.

• In individual therapy, a therapist who is a psychologist, psychiatrist (a psychologist who is also a medical doctor), or social worker works with you one-on-one.

- Family therapy is geared to help you understand your relationships with your family. Often, family members are involved. Understanding these relationships is important because unresolved issues can complicate your recovery. It is crucial if abuse is at the root of your eating disorder.
- Group therapy is shared therapy sessions with several people who share the same eating disorder. Sharing can help you see that you are not alone with this problem.

Healthy Eating Habits

Recovering from an eating disorder means learning healthier eating habits. Eating habits don't change overnight—it takes time and a lot of hard work. Your doctor or counselor may suggest that you keep a food diary so that you remain aware of how, when, where, and what you eat. You may meet with a dietician, who can help you plan meals that give you the right amount of nutrients and calories. Speaking with a registered dietitian or nutritionist at your school or family clinic about food and nutrition will help you understand why your body needs food, vitamins, and minerals to function properly. You'll learn why your body needs fat to stay healthy, too. In addition, you will learn that eating a variety of foods is healthy and that eating in response to hunger, rather than emotional needs, will help you reach your goals. A registered dietitian can help you relearn normal eating patterns.

You'll learn about portion control, keeping food stored out of sight, and not going to the grocery store when you're

Learning about nutritious foods, portion control, and meal planning is a critical part of recovery from an eating disorder. Listening to your body's hunger and fullness signals is another important skill to improve on for a favorable outcome.

hungry. You'll also learn more positive ways to deal with loneliness, anxiety, boredom, anger, frustration, and other emotions, and how to reward yourself with things other than food.

Most important, you will learn to listen to your body and trust its innate hunger and fullness signals. This inherent ability to self-regulate what, when, and how much you eat is called intuitive eating. You need to learn about hunger, appetite, and satisfaction, and trust your body to know when it's full. And you need to see food as an ally, rather than something that you should avoid, reject, or devour without thought.

The Recovery Process

Eating disorders can permanently damage the body, and a person may need hospitalization. The person can also die from an eating disorder. Even with professional help, the recovery process can be long and difficult, but many people do recover and go on to live successful, healthy lives.

The sooner the disorder is diagnosed and treated, the better the recovery outcome will be.

If you are struggling with an eating disorder, successful recovery depends on one person: you. Although it takes medical professionals, family, and friends to help you get better, only you can decide to start the recovery process and continue it.

Here are a few things you need to do to truly recover:

- Take part fully in your treatment plan and follow the instructions of your doctor, nutritionist, and therapist. Keep all appointments with your medical and health team, and never lie or hold back information when reporting what you've been doing.
- Be able to function independently in day-to-day living and show that you can cope with any problems or emotional stress that life brings.
- Keep your weight within 5 pounds (2.3 kilograms) of your assigned target weight. If your weight begins to drop (or rise, if you've had problems with bingeing in the past) for any reason, you need to get help right away.

The Danger of Relapse

Relapse is always a danger with eating disorders. That's why anytime there is the slightest hint that you are returning to destructive eating habits, you need to contact your doctor and therapist immediately.

Regardless of the eating disorder, the symptoms of relapse are very similar and may include the following:

- Gaining or losing 5 pounds (2.3 kg) or more from the maintenance weight range
- Increases in addictive behavior, whether that involves food, exercise, drugs, or alcohol
- A sudden or sharp decrease in appetite or ability to eat
- An episode of purging, along with renewed use of laxatives, diuretics, diet pills, or enemas
- A dramatic change in sleeping patterns—either sleeping more than usual or suddenly being unable to sleep

Write in a Journal

As you begin to incorporate changes in your life, you may find that keeping a journal is a good way to see how you've progressed. Your journal is a place that is all yours. It's a place to record your thoughts and feelings. It's a good idea, however, to pay attention to negative talk. The point of keeping a journal is to identify the things that trigger negative feelings. If you are having negative feelings, try to counter them with positive statements. Try to remember that your goal is to change your focus and work on developing a positive body image and self-image.

Have Patience with Yourself

Creating and maintaining a healthy body image and self-image are lifelong, full-time projects. It's exciting to discover who you are and what you are capable of doing.

Writing in a journal or blog is essential for seeing how far you've come in your recovery process and how special you really are. Your record can help you remember all the important, positive things in your life, your goals, and your dreams for the future.

Don't think that you are alone in your self-building project. Many people can help you—your family, friends, teachers, and fellow workers. You have nothing to lose but your old poor self-image. You will gain more of who you really are.

Have patience with yourself. Even though you are not perfect, you can be excellent. You are a valuable human being who is in the process of becoming everything you are meant to be.

anorexia nervosa An eating disorder in which a person has an intense fear of getting fat, refuses to eat, and keeps losing weight.

antidepressant A drug prescribed by a doctor to treat depression.

bingeing Rapid eating of large amounts of food—2,000 calories or more—during a short period of time.

body image The way you perceive your body and how you think others perceive your body.

bulimia An eating disorder in which someone eats a lot and then purges the food.

calorie A unit to measure the energy-producing value of food.

compulsive Relating to feeling psychologically unable to resist performing or doing things.

depression Feelings of sadness and hopelessness that last a long period of time.

gene The basic unit of inheritance in cells.

laxative A pill or liquid that brings on a bowel movement.

psychologist A specialist in the scientific study of human behavior who treats problems of the mind.

purge To get rid of food suddenly and harshly, usually by vomiting, exercise, or laxatives.

self-esteem Confidence, self-respect, or satisfaction with oneself.

self-image The way you see and think of yourself.

therapist A person trained to help patients recover from illness or injury.

About-Face
P.O. Box 77665
San Francisco, CA 94107
(415) 839-6779
Web site: http://www.about-face.org
About-Face promotes positive self-respect in girls and
women of all ages, sizes, races, and backgrounds by
helping them understand and oppose harmful media
messages that influence self-esteem and body image.

Alliance for Eating Disorders Awareness
P.O. Box 2562
West Palm Beach, FL 33402
(866) 662-1235
Web site: http://www.allianceforeatingdisorders.com
This organization helps young people and adults learn
about eating disorders and the positive effects of a
healthy body image.

Anorexia Nervosa and Related Eating Disorders, Inc.
(ANRED)
Web site: http://www.anred.com
The ANRED is a nonprofit group that is affiliated with
the National Eating Disorders Association (NEDA).
It provides information about eating disorders, pre-
vention, treatment, and recovery.

Bulimia/Anorexia Nervosa Association (BANA)
2109 Ottawa Street, Suite 400
Windsor, ON N8Y 1R8

Canada
(519) 969-2112
Web site: http://www.bana.ca
The BANA is a community-based Canadian organization
for eating disorders, health, and wellness.

Eating Disorders Clinic, Inc.
121 Willowdale Avenue, Suite 205
North York, ON M2N 6A3
Canada
(416) 483-0956
Web site: http://www.eatingdisorders.ca
The Eating Disorders Clinic, Inc., is committed to helping
individuals and their families deal with and recover
from eating disorders.

National Association of Anorexia Nervosa and Associated
Disorders, Inc. (ANAD)
P.O. Box 640
Naperville, IL 60566
(630) 577-1333; helpline (630) 577-1330
Web site: http://www.anad.org
The ANAD provides help and information about various
eating disorders, treatment options and effectiveness,
and support groups.

National Eating Disorders Association (NEDA)
165 West 46th Street
New York, NY 10036
(212) 575-6200; helpline (800) 931-2237

Web site: http://www.nationaleatingdisorders.org
The NEDA works to prevent eating disorders and provides
    materials on prevention and weight issues.

National Institute of Mental Health (NIMH)
6001 Executive Boulevard, Room 8184, MSC 9663
Bethesda, MD 20892
(866) 615-6464
Web site: http://www.nimh.nih.gov
The NIMH helps people learn about all aspects of mental
    health, including eating disorders.

Web Sites

Due to the changing nature of Internet links, Rosen
Publishing has developed an online list of Web sites
related to the subject of this book. This site is updated
regularly. Please use this link to access the list:

http://www.rosenlinks.com /tmh/sied

Allman, Toney. *Eating Disorders* (Hot Topics). Farmington Hills, MI: Lucent Books, 2010.

Bowman, Mary. *Relate: Self-Esteem & Body Image*. Findlay, OH: Relate Publishing, 2010.

Cooperman, Sheila A. *Living with Eating Disorders* (Teen's Guides). New York, NY: Facts On File, 2009.

Firth, Lisa. *Body Image and Self-Esteem*. Cambridge, UK: Independence Publishers, 2009.

Gillard, Arthur. *Eating Disorders* (Issues That Concern You). Farmington Hills, MI: Greenhaven Press, 2010.

Hefner, Keith, and Laura Longhine, eds. *Through Thick and Thin: Teens Write About Obesity, Eating Disorders, and Self-Image*. New York, NY: Youth Communication, New York Center, 2009.

Lawton, Sandra Augustyn. *Eating Disorders Information for Teens: Health Tips About Anorexia, Bulimia, Binge Eating, and Other Eating Disorders*. 2nd ed. Detroit, MI: Omnigraphics, 2009.

Littman, Sarah Darer. *Purge*. Reprint ed. New York, NY: Scholastic, 2010.

MacKay, Jennifer. *Anorexia and Bulimia* (Diseases & Disorders). Farmington Hills, NY: Lucent Books, 2009.

Nelson, Tammy. *What's Eating You? A Workbook for Teens with Anorexia, Bulimia, and other Eating Disorders* (Instant Help Book for Teens). Oakland, CA: Instant Help Books, 2008.

Roizen, Michael F., and Mehmet C. Oz. *You: The Owner's Manual for Teens: A Guide to a Healthy Body and Happy Life*. New York, NY: Free Press, 2011.

Shivack, Nadia. *Inside Out: Portrait of an Eating Disorder*. New York, NY: Atheneum Books, 2007.

About the Authors

Rita Smith is a retired medical social worker and writer who lives in Michigan.

Vanessa Baish writes nonfiction books for young adults and lives in New York.

Edward Willett has written numerous books on science and health topics for young adults; he resides in Regina, Saskatchewan, Canada.

Stephanie Watson is a writer and editor who is based in Atlanta, Georgia. She has written or contributed to more than a dozen health and science books, including works on eating disorders.

Photo Credits